SB1005

Winds of Worship

12 Hymn Arrangements for One or More Wind Players
Arranged by Stan Pethel

CONTENTS

Immortal, Invisible	3
Take My Life and Let It Be	10
Joyful, Joyful, We Adore Thee	17
Near to the Heart of God	23
Praise the Lord Who Reigns Above	28
Love Lifted Me	34
Like a River Glorious	41
I Will Sing of the Mercies	48
Savior, Like a Shepherd Lead Us	53
Higher Ground	58
My Jesus, I Love Thee	63
He's Got the Whole World in His Hands	68

Shawnee Press, Inc.
A Subsidiary of Music Sales Corporation
Distribution Center: 445 Bellvale Road • Chester, NY 10918

Visit Shawnee Press Online at www.shawneepress.com

Arr. Copyright © 2006 Shawnee Press, Inc.
International Copyright Secured. All Rights Reserved.
SOLE SELLING AGENT: SHAWNEE PRESS, INC., NASHVILLE, TN 37212

PREFACE

Winds of Worship was designed to allow for maximum flexibility of use. The uses range from full ensemble to solo instrument and piano. All of the arrangements will work with or without piano, just start at the first double bar or the pickups to the first double bar.

Here are some options:

1. Solo instrument and piano or track. The piano/score book works as accompaniment for all instruments as does the accompaniment CD.

2. Multiple instruments and piano or track. Just have one instrument play the solo part and the other(s) the ensemble part along with the piano or accompaniment CD. Use more players on the solo part if needed to project the melody.

3. For instruments only, with no piano or CD accompaniment, these combinations will work:

    a. Brass Quartet – trumpet 1 & 2 with trombone 1 & 2 parts will stand alone. Start at the first double bar.

    b. Brass Quintet or Brass Sextet – For quintet use trumpet 1 & 2, horn, trombone 1, and tuba. For sextet add trombone 2. Start at the double bar.

    c. Other ensemble combinations. As long as trumpet 1 & 2 and trombone 1 & 2 are covered, the other parts will only add to the fullness of the ensemble. Piano adds even more and fills out the harmony. For instruments only start at the double bar, with piano starting at the beginning.

    d. Remember these instrumental substitutions. Violins and oboes can play or double the flute part. Clarinets can play or double the trumpet parts. Cellos, bassoons, and baritones can play the trombone part. Bass trombone players may want to try the tuba part as well. The tuba part can also be covered by a bass setting from an electric keyboard to add depth to the sound.

The difficulty level for these arrangements range from grade 2 ½ to 3. They are good lengths for preludes, offertories, and featured instrumental performance in both church services as well as church or school concerts. Most are also in good vocal range should you choose to add choral or congregational singing at appropriate places.

Best wishes with these arrangements in your area of musical ministry. Let us know at Shawnee Press if you find them useful, and what else we can do to assist with your instrumental needs.

Stan Pethel

Immortal, Invisible

TRADITIONAL WELSH HYMN MELODY
Arranged by STAN PETHEL

Arr. Copyright © 2006 Shawnee Press, Inc.
International Copyright Secured. All Rights Reserved.
SOLE SELLING AGENT: SHAWNEE PRESS, INC., NASHVILLE, TN 37212

Take My Life and Let It Be

Music by HENRY A. César MALAN
Arranged by STAN PETHEL

Arr. Copyright © 2006 Shawnee Press, Inc.
International Copyright Secured. All Rights Reserved.
SOLE SELLING AGENT: SHAWNEE PRESS, INC., NASHVILLE, TN 37212

Joyful, Joyful, We Adore Thee

Music by **LUDWIG van BEETHOVEN**
Arranged by **STAN PETHEL**

Arr. Copyright © 2006 Shawnee Press, Inc.
International Copyright Secured. All Rights Reserved.
SOLE SELLING AGENT: SHAWNEE PRESS, INC., NASHVILLE, TN 37212

22

Near to the Heart of God

23

Music by CLELAND B. McAFEE
Arranged by STAN PETHEL

Arr. Copyright © 2006 Shawnee Press, Inc.
International Copyright Secured. All Rights Reserved.
SOLE SELLING AGENT: SHAWNEE PRESS, INC., NASHVILLE, TN 37212

24

26

Praise the Lord Who Reigns Above

FOUNDRY COLLECTION, 1742
Arranged by **STAN PETHEL**

30

33

34

Love Lifted Me

Music by **HOWARD E. SMITH**
Arranged by **STAN PETHEL**

Arr. Copyright © 2006 Shawnee Press, Inc.
International Copyright Secured. All Rights Reserved.
SOLE SELLING AGENT: SHAWNEE PRESS, INC., NASHVILLE, TN 37212

35

38

Like a River Glorious

Music by **JAMES MOUNTAIN**
Arranged by **STAN PETHEL**

Arr. Copyright © 2006 Shawnee Press, Inc.
International Copyright Secured. All Rights Reserved.
SOLE SELLING AGENT: SHAWNEE PRESS, INC., NASHVILLE, TN 37212

44

I Will Sing of the Mercies

Arr. Copyright © 2006 Shawnee Press, Inc.
International Copyright Secured. All Rights Reserved.
SOLE SELLING AGENT: SHAWNEE PRESS, INC., NASHVILLE, TN 37212

51

Savior, Like a Shepherd Lead Us

Music by **WILLIAM B. BRADBURY**
Arranged by **STAN PETHEL**

Arr. Copyright © 2006 Shawnee Press, Inc.
International Copyright Secured. All Rights Reserved.
SOLE SELLING AGENT: SHAWNEE PRESS, INC., NASHVILLE, TN 37212

54

56

Higher Ground

Music by **CHARLES H. GABRIEL**
Arranged by **STAN PETHEL**

Arr. Copyright © 2006 Shawnee Press, Inc.
International Copyright Secured. All Rights Reserved.
SOLE SELLING AGENT: SHAWNEE PRESS, INC., NASHVILLE, TN 37212

60

62

My Jesus, I Love Thee

Music by ADONIRAM J. GORDON
Arranged by STAN PETHEL

Arr. Copyright © 2006 Shawnee Press, Inc.
International Copyright Secured. All Rights Reserved.
SOLE SELLING AGENT: SHAWNEE PRESS, INC., NASHVILLE, TN 37212

64

65

66

He's Got the Whole World in His Hands

TRADITIONAL SPIRITUAL
Arranged by **STAN PETHEL**